WHEN I WAS BORN

NANDINI SHRIVASTAVA

Made with ♥ on the Notion Press Platform
www.notionpress.com

TO ALL THE SMALL DREAMS WHICH BRINGS THE
BIGGEST HAPPINESS

Contents

Contents

Contents

Preface

THE WORK THAT I HAVE CLUBED IN HERE IS SOMETHING THAT I HAVE BEEN WRITTING SINCE PAST 5 YEARS. MY EVERY POEM CONTAINS THE EMOTION AND MORAL AND I HAVE DONE MY BEST TO LET MY READERS UNDERSTAND THE DEEP MEANINGS BEHIND THEM. FROM MOTIVATING TO INCLUDING THE DARKEST EMOTIONS, I BELIEVE I HAVE BOTTLED UP EVERY KIND OF EMOTION I HAVE EVERY FELT. AS A YOUNG POET, I AM NOT CONFIDENT ENOUGH TO SAY THIS IS THE BEST PIECE BUT I SURE HAVE LEARNT TO BE A BETTER POET EACH TIME I WROTE SOMETHING WHICH HAD FLAWS AND HOPE TO WRITE THE BETTER ONES IN FUTURE.

Acknowledgements

I have been writing since I was 12. that 12-year-old Nandini never was confident enough to even think about publishing her book at the age of 16. I just kept on writing poems because I loved writing them. but slowly-slowly as I kept on penning the words and filling my diary up, the unthinkable became my dream and when I finished my first diary filled with poems, I was sure I am one day going to hold a book of mine. and so did writing this acknowledgment letter for my books became a dream too.

from that 12-year-old to today me publishing this, on this road, I was not alone. though I walked on my own feet I had people who made sure I keep walking and did not stop. I will definitely start by jotting down my gratitude toward my parents. They have given me all that I wanted and have been the best parents. They have blessed me with a lot that I simply don't deserve because I have not been an as wonderful child as the wonderful parents they are. But thank you for always keeping my wishes and needs as your priority. Thank you for blessing me with extreme love and care and nourishing me with education, knowledge, and values.

I would dearly wanna give the credit to my best friends. they were the ones who made sure I never stop. they made sure that I won't doubt myself. they were the ones who loved me when I hated myself and made me believe in all my strengths. thank you so much Rhythm and thank you so much, Ritu, for always being there for me, supporting me, being happy in my happiness, and standing right beside me in my wars. thank you for cheering me on when I was miserable, for wiping off my tears. thank you so much for reading my poems, and judging them the right way. thank you for telling me that I am capable of everything. you guys are the greatest gift in my life, for real. I for sure owe you a universe.

I thank my teachers from the very bottom of my heart. their support, guidance, love, and help have always been a boost for me and I can't even imagine myself as an individual if they haven't been in my life. thank you so much for every bit of knowledge and guidance you have ever given me. thank you so much for always being so patient and helpful. I would like to extend my gratitude to my school. thank you for always encouraging me and making me a confident individual.

Last but not the least, my greatest thank is to my god. thank you for keeping your upon me and giving me your strength and guidance. my belief in you has always given me hope for a better future.

POEMS

1. US

Here in lies,
Our sorrows and pain.
Our grief, our revenge.
soaking our hearts,
making it drought up,
but just a sense of nature
needed to grow the flowers.

feel alive again,
throw out your anger,
focus on the good,
and let it grow your power.
I rip off those layers in my heart,
let it enjoy the rest,
focus on what really makes you well.

remind me oh mother,
I come for your comfort,
the scent of the rain,
and the way you make me blossom.

2. First Drops

Wake up your spirits
the raindrops are falling again,
the air is fresh,
bringing heaven again.

feel the comfort,
as it falls on the ground,
the winds are alarming,
revive the joy under.

it's the first day of rain,
of the year, I await.
washing up pains,
see how these droplets,
make me feel angelic.

3. Moonlight

Walking in the moonlight,
I see the colors of the night,
I hear the soul,
That is deep,
I want to dig into their weep.
Walking in the stargaze,
Loving things that are with me,
I weep for the things I don't have,
It's the nature of every being.

Indulge yourself in the Moon's beauty,
Highlight your silver lining
Let it take your sorrows,
cause' when I am running from myself
my every victory feels like a death

4. Today's Rains

The day of thunder today was,
which brought heavy black clouds.
and all the heavy raindrops were falling
all over the ground.

and the windchime is ringing
alarming so hard
'The Monsoon's here'
its shout is heard by all.

the big droplets of heavy rain,
captured my city
and the clouds roared so loud
that it made everyone believe.

today I saw,
I witnessed that the rain's perilous
the one which was my comfort,
today looked dangerous.

the winds flew so fast
to carry the rain with them

NANDINI SHRIVASTAVA

they made my view blurry,
how fast it was.

the doors were shut loud enough,
loud to make them all hear.
the lightning was so fast
strong enough to let the strong ones shatter

the small and weak plants
were thrown out of the soil.
the street lights were shut now
which once shined bright.

the sky which is ocean blue
was now deep dark
the dense clouds
freaked all hearts.

the view was perilous enough,
that it felt like the god of
wind, rain, and thunder
was on the earth for real.

so sonorous it was,
yet my heart felt calm.
it was at least better than
the hazard better than us,

soon the loud winds were over,
but the rain was still falling.
no matter how strong they were,
they always made me fall for them.

these events bring freshness around,
and it has always freed
the darkness which was caged in my heart,
deep beyond.

5. Horizon

The twinkling stars,
I let them shine,
I let them enter,
And glow up wide.
Come to the top,
You'll soon be on the horizon,
Diming slowly,
Vanishing faster.
I wait for you,
You'll rise next,
You'll come,
I don't care about the rest.
Let me endure your absence,
Because you'll rise,
And life will again make sense.
Again, I'll try to be wise.

6. Serene

All through the night,
When the world fell quiet
When I am alone
And there is just
The moon and the soul of mine.

His shine from the height,
Struck my heart so tight,
And its color so pure white
Heals my soul, every night!

7. Colorless Tints

If only my tears had colors,
They should've seen the tints,
When I roughly rubbed them off my cheeks,

For all it takes
To make them believe,
That I am set off just fine
Is lifting the corner of my lips up high.

if only did my eyes could scale
all the water it rained,
I would drown and die in that

for all it takes to make it vanish
is a piece of tissue in my pocket
and covering my eyes with a layer of glasses.

8. Embrace

Embrace me when I'm dull
please feel my essence
my existence,
and my feelings that are consistent

don't make me fade away
the smile that I bear,
I have no intention to
wear the crown given.

let me just survive,
let me endure it,
don't step in between
and block what coming

I am a preacher of the dark,
let me head to the sun
please don't make me
imagine the worse.

sitting behind the untold,
let my heart shower,

I don't expect to understand
just try it once.

or leave me behind,
I won't bother.
I'll pave the way myself.
please don't gather.

9. The Shadows In My Life

sitting behind the table
the shadows scares me.
they tell me to be certain,
the way that I feel.
shedding my tears sometimes,
but learning to fight,
they want me to be ordinary.

my nurturers are under pressure,
raising me up in the same way
while expecting me not tobe like the world.
the shadows of my world.
capture my heart, hits me daily
And stains deep under

10. The Car Drive

I went in my car on a drive,
a rainy day when
I wanted to make my soul alive

the daily drama was out of my mind
towards the soul of nature, I arrived.
situations that were contrived,
earlier that day,
I forgot and filled my day
with happiness.
it felt like,
I was alive again

11. The Monsoon's Arrival

The rain is here
By The first monsoon winds,
Bringing freshness all around,
And makes the leaves swing.

The wind chimes are
Alarming its arrival,
and the wetness of the soil,
Makes me feel wondered.

When the land was enough dry,
And the body sweats,
The rain brings the cold breezes
And the cloudy days.

The rain splashes on my face,
And blows my hair away,
Oh, the monsoon is back,
And back in the cool days.

NANDINI SHRIVASTAVA

The thunderstorm is here,
With the lightning speed,
And I love the way nature tells
The arrival of the rainy weeks.

It makes me feel fresh,
Oh, the cool winds!
It was sweating hot hours ago,
But the air is clear now,
And I rejoice its commence.

New hopes are being brought,
And the lesson to be strong!
There is no space for the weak ones,
The wind will blow them off!!

Only the ones with braveheart
Can survive the sound of thunder,
Let all the weaklings
Hide behind and let'em block their ears.

And I stand on my balcony,
With the hairs spread around,
Feeling the breezes of the wind,
Because my heart rejoices,
The monsoon's arrival

12. A Bird

Mommy and daddy decided to keep a bird,
A little bird was brought,
Beautiful wings it had,
Like a little baby,
They kept.
And she lived a life with no bad.
Mommy and daddy fed her,
Get her new things,
Toys to play,
And love to offer
And endless care.
They got her cage,
A Cage she thought is love,
She lived a life,
Thinking so,
Well, nothing was wrong though.
When the seasons fall off
One by one, day by day,
She got older,
They feed her more,
They got her more,
Mommy and daddy,

Loved her more.
But still, they were anxious,
Were worried about when she'll grow up.
A bird gets lost, when it grows,
Were their concerns.
They forgot to change the cage,
Maybe their innocence
Even when the bird grew up.
It was no more the place she loved,
It was something,
Which bounded her.
And one day she got the chance,
Got the day to rock,
Nobody was seeing her,
She flew off.
Mommy and daddy didn't knew,
Didn't knew when she flew,
All they're left to do,
Is to remember her,
Coz a flown bird,
Never returns..

13. 21st Century Friendships

The world has changed,
So does emotions,
But yet friendship is unique,
Feelings unchanged,

A casual emoji,
But a friend can feel,
The feeling behind it,
Sweet or contrary.

A zoom call,
An amazon gift,
But yet feelings unchanged.

May the world is,
Extremely evolved,
But the feeling of a friend is
Never lost.

Because the friend is

The one we choose,
And there's nothing
We could refuse...

• 21 •

14. Death

You lay down the coffin,
With the crown on your head,
You stab your head against,
You're helpless.
You dig down the ground,
You lay the box in.
With power in your hand,
You're still helpless.
Bury them off,
You have no choice,
Cover it off,
Your red flickering eyes.
Set the ice on fire,
Melt it down to hell,
Cover the box up,
With the same soil
Same soil as the one who begs.
Coz, even if you've got,
The throw to sit-on,
You're still a pity little human
Bound by the rules of the god...

15. The Midnights

I was not what I am,
I was never busy,
I was never afraid,
And my life was never dizzy.

See, I stand here today,
I am,
I am a lot different
My life is now,
So incoherent
It is so irrelevant
To happiness

Yes, it is changed,
And the easiness
Of life is so drained.
I find no one blame!
No one to say,
Say out my words
And I am so being
One of the nerds.

WHEN I WAS BORN

It was,
It was never difficult,
It has turned hell sometimes,
And I find no cause.

I had a smile,
Always upright
I felt happy,
And full of delight.
See me now,
Locked in a room,
Have fussed my feelings,
Have unsaid words,
In my heart deep.

Does it happen with everyone,
Or is it only,
On this dark wood,
With forked roads,
For me!

16. Soul Of Mine

All through the night,
When the world fell quiet
When I am alone
And there is just
The moon and the soul of mine.

His shine from the height,
Struck my heart so tight,
And it's color is so pure white
Heals my soul, every night!

17. The Half-lit Moon

I saw him,
I saw him half-lit,
A yellow tint,
And in perfect shape.

Hiding some scars,
Showing some of them.
Letting you witness,
It's weekly games.

He shines bright,
Even when he's a crecent,
He is still the king,
No matter how small or dim.

His white pearl light,
Is the way he shines,
With twinkles behind,
And spreading love
All night...

18. Animals

The beings roaming,
The one called dumb,
And treated like slaves
Lost and survived,
Feeling suffocated, in their cages
And are afraid.
Spare something,
For these unsaid,
Have some mercy,
They also feel the same.
Humans have lost humanity,
We've ruined everything,
Please give yourself a clarity,
That they aren't our property.

19. My Dear

Moon, my dear
Thank you so much
For witnessing my every second
And to choose to listen
My cry.
No matter how much I try
But there is no one
To listen that I am right.
And then I rejoice,
I wipe my tears
Because you are here
Always shining so bright
To make me feel
That there is someone
To listen my every cry.

20. Listener

i stand here alone,
with millions of words,
no one to listen
cause' they're busy
with their work.

i wanna share the facts I know.
and I listen to them too.
but I think they are not interested
in what I think.
they're busy on something
more important.

i feel alone,
I feel helpless sometimes
like there's no one to listen
neither my words nor my cries.

but I know that there is
still someone to listen
to hear what I speak,
the one in sky.

the one that shines bright.
he's my listener.
when my own people are busy.
doing something right...

21. The Girl

dark across the blackness around the lights of the city have lit the ground. And among all the rushes lives a girl with benevolence. the girl, dreams day and night, dusk and dawn, and every time cause' she waits for the world to listen to her side of the story and greatness. and she practices being that every second. and for long she talks, she gossips with the twinkling stars cause' she knows she isn't alone, even if she's behind those bars. as her fate bought her here and no she's not the one to blame. and she knows her maker's here for they will make her life like the one she deserves...

22. Pearl'em

Randomly I pick,
I pick any pearl,
I pick any stone,
I choose them randomly.
I pearl'em in a neckpiece,
A piece of necklace
And It looks
That what I've choose,
Have choose them randomly,
But though they don't know,
The people that it wasn't randomly.
The truth of them,
That they were destined,
They were destined to be together,
To be stacked one after another.
And it's what I've learned.
That coincidence is nothing,
Nothing is that and it's an illusion.
Because the truth is destiny,
And everything else is there for an confusion.

23. Blooming

My feelings bloomed like a flower did
the bud was visible
but the fragrance reached
my senses today.
what else do I do?
no, I can't hide'em.
just can put up a blank face,
and let my heart race...

24. Kindest Touch

The kindest touch
is of the god and soul,
the peace is utmost,
things are wonderful.
but it's your heart you should obey
and don't be trolled

25. Life

Life is beautiful,
Yes, sometimes.
But
Sometimes worse than,
Our imagination
Awkward
And with no validation.
It comes
Without any expectations
And ruins life with no doubt
And no hopes for future.

26. I Wanna Write

I see myself
In a fighting ring
With millions of rivals
And a sword in my hand
I wanna fight
I wanna tell
My every feeling
I ever felt
I wanna shout
And way too loud
With my works
Not with my mouth
I wanna show
My every move
I wanna prove
And say my haters a big No,
I wanna fight
I wanna tell everyone
That I deserve the right
I wanna fight
I wanna fight
I wanna write

NANDINI SHRIVASTAVA

I wanna write

27. When I Tried To Call A Person

The person with whom ,
I wanted to connect ,
Was lost somewhere..
I regret !!!
Dedicated for others I wasted my time,
I never realised,
With the most important person,
I compromised !!
I made a call to myself,
The person was busy on another call,
Oh no ! There's nothing left.
The time is gone ,
I regret !!!

28. The Sun Moon Love

The Moon that lits up,

The scary nights.

And the sun that,

Shines so bright.

The one which gives,

Moments of peace,

And the other,

The inspiration to shine.

Their love has been so strong,

And it's existence is so long,

That we are really,

So fond of.

Their grace is,

So upon us,

That they boost up,

Even the most wuss.

Their existence and love,

Has made us possible,

And have taught us,

That they're capable to make or destroy us.

29. If I Fail To See Tomorrow

If I fail to see tomorrow,
Undoubtedly, I'll be in sorrow,
Till my last breath,
I'll be thankful till my last breath..

If I fail to see tomorrow,
I'll face death with full courage,
And to Make sure
I don't make someone upset..

If I fail to see tomorrow,
I would give my things To needy,
I would donate for them ,
who are bleedy ..

If I fail to see tomorrow,
I may apologize to the ones ,
With whom i was sarcastic,
And to the ones,
I made them cry...

If I fail to see tomorrow,

30. It's Special

ITS A DAY OF THUNDER,
AND THE BLACK SKY,
WHEN THE WATER IS,
FALLING FROM THE HEIGHT..
THE SOUND OF PITTER-PATTER,
AMAZE MY SOUL.
BUT THE HARSH THUNDER VOICE,
FREAKS ALL HEARTS...

WHEN THE SPLASHES OF RAIN,
TOUCHES MY SKIN,
I FEEL LIKE,
BEING IN HEAVEN..
THE COOL RUNNING WIND,
BLOWS OFF MY SMOOTH HAIR.
IT MAKES THE LEAVES DANCE,
WHICH ARE WELOMING THE RAIN..

NOW I COULD SEE
THE CREEPY INSECTS ALL AROUND,
WHICH PEEPS OUT,
FROM THE INSIDE GROUND..

AND YES, ONCE AGAIN,
I'M IN A SCRAPE,
I CAN'T DECIDE,
IS IT MY FAVORITE ?

ITS BEEN CONFUSING,
SINCE I'VE BORN,
WELL, I CANT DO ANYTHING,
BUT THAT'S NOT REGRETING...

PERHAPS, IF IT WONT BE,
THE ONE MOST ADORED BY ME,
BUT THE WINDS, THE SPLASHES REMINDS ME,
THAT'S ITS SPECIAL !!!

31. Confused Hope

Lost,

I am,

Felling lazy..

Confused,

And pissing up ..

In my mind...

Incomplete

I am,

In between,

Negativity.

Don't know when I'll reach ,

The doors of positivity

Searching,

I am,

For better things,,

I pray to god,

I may get'em soon

32. The Colors Of My Feathers

Across my inner universe
Which lies beneath my soul
I wander here and there
Finding the way in my life's bowl...

I'm confused, desperately
Asking for answers repeatedly
In hope, may my god reply
I've faith because on him I rely.

The colors of my feather,
Sometimes have hue of greys
But things will be fine again
I pray..

Life is black, white, and grey,,
I wish I could relax on my bed,,
Thinking of situations that aren't in my hand,,
I wish my life would turn as bright as red...

33. Overcome

A pleasant day while,
Sitting on a street bench,
I saw a girl yelling on one,
By saying overcome...

It struck my mind,
Like a,
A bow and arrow,
And I thought about it in a sorrow..
How could one can overcome,
Everyone fears,
Man or one...

Just trust yourself,
Have faith,
Face them,
Don't get scare..
If you can't just overcome,
How could you love,
Live or learn..

Just face the fears,

Don't scare..
Just trust yourself,
Have faith..

34. They'll Grow

Hidden in the cloudy shed,
I couldn't see the twinkling stars
Oh, it's gonna rain!
Wow, could feel the windy blaze
I could see the weak movement,
Branches of trees
And the electric wires
Swinging
The sky is the majority of
Greyish blue.
But extracts of white too
Now it is visible
What I was searching for
Peeped from the cover of
Blues grey cloudy fur
Now I found
My heart smiled
Seeing the king of the night sky,
He vanished..
And yes,
I could see
The leaves,

Eagerly waiting for
The pitter-patter drops..
The winds are blowing
I am too
Seeking the way out
From the clouds glowing..
Oh! Because of the wind
The clouds blew off.
Now the sky is clear
And I am able to seek off.
The trees,
The ground
Have to wait a little more
To calm down their thirst
Or someone should water them,
They'll grow.

35. At 12

i know i'm bad,
i know i suck
cause' everytime
there's something messed up.
and everyday is like
a reunion
to my lonely shit
that I've become.
and I no longer wish
to be someone nice.
i no longer wish
to be someone people expect.
i wanna rage out mad
wanna be a dark bad bitch
cause' the inner demons rule me
when the clock stuck twelve

36. Goal

Walking through this road of life,
One should have something to Achieve..
A goal should be set ,
To have a reason
To struggle wise.

Optimism is most important,,
To achieve what you wanted...
Love your goal with full determination.
And do remember,
That thing cannot happen without a strong motion..

All the way climbing up life mountain,
You will realize,
That it is more difficult then Mt Everest.
You don't get scare..
Because anything can be achieved
In this world and away...

37. You

My heart's in, deep on ignite
Coz, I am dancing, all night...
and I am flying, in my dreams like.
you're the one, holding me tight,
around

And when I see you, in that black shirt,
it's like seeing in front, my whole world
and when I miss you,
it's like a stone, that has been hit on
my love...

And I sit here gazing U night long,
no, I won't say, that I am fine now
Coz, baby all I crave and all ever I want
Is you...
Yea, it's you...

And all I dream, and all I search,
It's your presence and nothing much,
Coz, baby I'm crying, just hold me now..

WHEN I WAS BORN

it's your heart where I wanna belong

and I am staring at the moon now,
Because you are so far, still i wanna come now.
running through the dark woods, in the dark clouds,
and i wanna roll down to you now,
yea you now

and I am searching, for your every traces,
in my diary, and every places
and now I dream of, every moment.
I had you and now embrace.
yea, I wanna go back,
to all our dates when,.
I was smiling,...
with love curled in...

And how could I'd ever lose,
the very part, my heart produces,
coz u exist now, in my every breath,
and you'll always be my, till my death
my end......

Don't worry I won't run to the ground,

I plan on flying always now...
With you in my arms, all night long..
Through the cities, in burning stars...
Coz, baby all I dream of is you.
Yea you...

And I wander through these dark wood,
Looking weird, like a selfish fool...
Coz, baby all I want is you...
Yes, you...
And all I pray, all I ever ask,
Is your smile, and all your love..
I know I messed up... And that's too much
Coz, baby I am sorry, I won't lie.
I'll make it up with all my life...
I'll love you to the moon and far.
Just please come to me back

38. Rules Of Life

Walking through the woods of life
the twists and turns
and the list of guides,
I urge to say,
I try with my might
obeying the rules of life
living off like a newborn turtle,
ups and downs all in a cycle
bound by time,
the principle we all obey.
and that's what
limits a mortal

COUPLETS AND QUOTES

39. World

"I am lost in the memories, I am lost in vain.
I am lost in the middle of nowhere.
between the ones I love, between the ones I care
and in between the ones I detest,
there's a world out there..."

40. Questions

"*and now that I am asking the questions again*

why are you refusing the answer, it

only takes a few words

and I'll be able to free my soul.

I'll have the courage to let myself roar.

and now that you've made me regret the

past decisions I've made, will it

ever be a concern in your head?

now that I hope to shine within my core."

41. Nights

"*And now that he's gone*

the night sky is darker.

now that he's gone.

the side stars are shining.

and now that he's gone

those star light isn't enough.

and he's gone,

who'll light up those streets where I wander"

42. Someone

" I have learned from the horrors
I have been taught by the demons
like everybody else,
have you been born as someone?"

43. Now

"*okay, so easy now?*
only seven months but
cozy now?
ah, it'll take a while.
or do you think it's gonna be like how it is now?"

44. Before

"FORE U GO DEEP DOWN INTO YOUR
THOUGHTS
AND DROWN IN THEM
YOU KNOW IT'S NOT GONNA END WELL.
STABBED BY THE ASSUMPTIONS,
IT'S BLEEDING WITH EMOTIONS.
BUT IS THE REALITY ANY DIFFERENT?"

45. Deapths

"I have been realizing the depths of the universe,
as infinity itself defines it
as the thoughts popping in my brain right now,
like the soul of the god itself creates it..."

46. Future

"*The sun's melting its colors,*
as I've painted my future,
and like how leisurely in a blink of an eye,
I no longer see the sun,
that is how I feel,
like I've triggered the bullet in the gun"

47. I Relate

"And now that I have heard the tune of the world
And now that I have seen what's ruled by the demons
And now that I have been to the places people talk about
And now that I've felt the things people write about
And now that I've gone through what's called Life
And now that I've read books that have never been written
And now that I've longed for things they've rapped about,
I can relate, no wonder."

48. Road Of Life

49. Love

<blockquote>
"Like a poem melting on a stove
have you ever seen
a fire burning in a
continental slope?"
</blockquote>

50. Worth

"*Existing as life as I have questioned the inanimates*

believing in the soul of them as I begin

accelerating my pace.

doubting god's this creation

does it really worth it?"

www.ingramcontent.com/pod-product-compliance
Lightning Source LLC
Chambersburg PA
CBHW061706130726

47996CB00006B/2187